# Enrichment Magazine

**TO THE DIRECTOR**

*This student folder contains nine study leaflets and the enrichment magazine. Open the staple to remove the leaflets. Distribute the leaflets as indicated in the leaders guide. The magazine should be distributed at the first session for use throughout the course.*


3558 S. Jefferson Ave.
St. Louis, MO 63118-3968



Written by Korey Maas

Edited by Edward Engelbrecht



This publication is available in braille, in large print, or on cassette tape for the visually impaired. Please allow 8 to 12 weeks for delivery. Write to the Library for the Blind, 1333 S. Kirkwood Road, St. Louis, MO 63122-7295; call 1-800-433-3954, ext. 1322; or e-mail to blind.library@lcms.org.

Manufactured in the U.S.A.

Cover illustration: Chris Ellison
Graphic design: Karen Pauls

IN THIS ISSUE ...

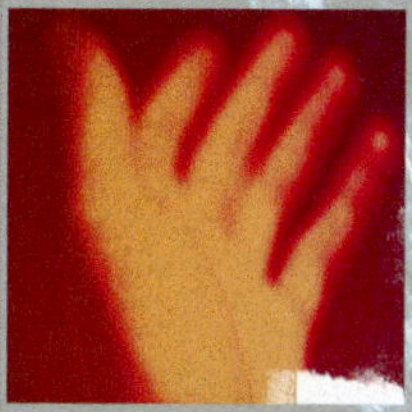

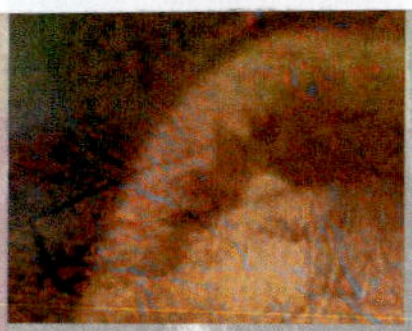



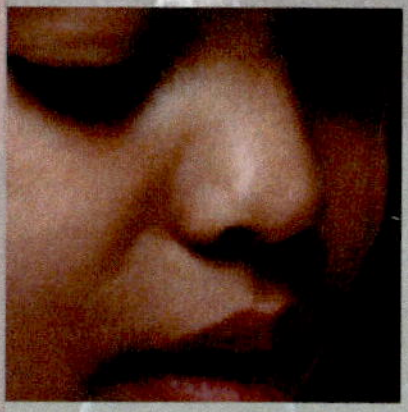



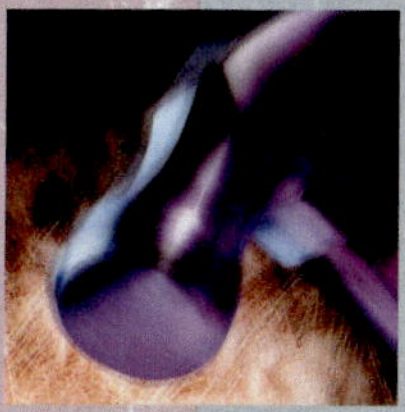

# THE MYSTERY OF HISTORY

SAINT LUKE BY GIUSTO DI GIOVANNI MENABUOI, FRESCO © BAPTISTRY OF THE CATHEDRAL, PADUA, ITALY/SUPERSTOCK

In 1905 the Spanish-born writer George Santayana gave one of the most-quoted reasons to study history. Just four years later, writer Elbert Hubbard gave one of the most-quoted reasons to ignore history. Santayana warned, "Those who cannot remember the past are condemned to repeat it." Hubbard griped, "Life is just one [blasted] thing after another."

You may agree or disagree with either of these opinions. But as you begin this study of the Book of Acts—the first church history—recognize that Acts provides more than a warning and more than just one thing after another. In Acts, St. Luke presents the mystery of history, the mystery of God's grace in Jesus Christ.

## Divine History

Rather than listing "one blasted thing after another," Luke outlines a dramatic story of one blessed thing after another. A broken band of disciples is restored to its original number and sent out with a mission. The good order of the church, threatened by disorganization and internal squabbling, was salvaged by the appointment of men to oversee daily administrative tasks. And countless individuals were rescued from the eternal consequences of sin as they heard the preaching of the Good News.

When Luke takes pen in hand, he writes with the assumptions of a historian. For example, in the prologue to his Gospel he writes, "Since I myself have carefully investigated everything from the beginning, it seemed good also to me to write an orderly account" (Luke 1:3). This he does. And in his second book—the Acts of the Apostles—he chronicles the first 30 years of the Christian church by summarizing the most important names, dates, places, and events. But far from the dry and dusty repetition of facts that characterizes so much historical writing, the narrative of Acts is infused with a sense of mystery. Tongues of fire hover unexpectedly overhead, crippled beggars rise to walk again, a blinding vision appears on a lonely road to Damascus. History and the mystery of God's grace meet here, and the results are no less startling or relevant for us than for those who took part in the divine drama that Luke records.

## Teaching by Example

Contemporary culture, which revels in the here and now, can sometimes forget that ancient history can indeed be relevant. History, unless one aspires to a tweed-wearing and pipe-smoking professorship, is quite frequently considered something only to be suffered in the confines of a classroom. But Luke took a different view. As an educated man and a Greek by birth, he probably held the view of learned Greeks, who understood history to be "philosophy teaching by example" (Dionysius).

Luke, of course, was no philosopher. The apostle Paul notes that he was a physician (Colossians 4:14). But when he took up his pen to write, Luke understood that the facts of his story were eternally relevant. They describe the ways of God with mankind and the workings of God in His church. History, Luke might have said, is theology teaching by example.

For example, what would a church look like when its members are one in heart and mind? Acts 4:32–36 tells us and prompts us even today to contemplate how well we reflect the fact that we have "one Lord, one faith, one baptism" (Ephesians 4:5). How does one effectively proclaim the Gospel in a multicultural world? This very twenty-first-century question is brilliantly answered again and again by the examples of the first-century preachers in Acts. What place do we have in our churches for the dregs of humanity, the drunks, the adulterers, even the murderers? Before answering that, we would do well to ask what place God had in *His* church for such people. A very poignant answer will be found in the example of Saul, the man who abetted the murder of Stephen the Deacon, but became the church's single greatest missionary.

## Prescription and Description

But history, even theology teaching by example, has its limitations; the emphasis on examples cannot be pressed too far. We will never assume, for instance, that modern Christians who do not sell their homes and give all their money to their pastors—as some early believers did—are less than ideal Christians. Nor is there any assumption in

Acts that Christians in all ages will speak in tongues (or, to the great relief of fire marshalls everywhere, that flames will descend when they gather for worship). History by its very nature is descriptive rather than prescriptive. While Luke faithfully describes what *did* happen in the early church, he does not necessarily prescribe what *must* happen in the church in all ages.

How then should we read the Book of Acts and understand the examples provided by those there described? Perhaps the author of the letter to the Hebrews gives us the best advice: "Consider the outcome of their way of life and imitate their faith. Jesus Christ is the same yesterday and today and forever" (Hebrews 13:7–8). This gets to the heart of the matter. Acts, where history and the mystery of God's grace meet, is salvation history. As the story of salvation, it is the story of faith. And this faith remains as relevant today as it did in the first century, because it is faith in the Christ, who does not change.

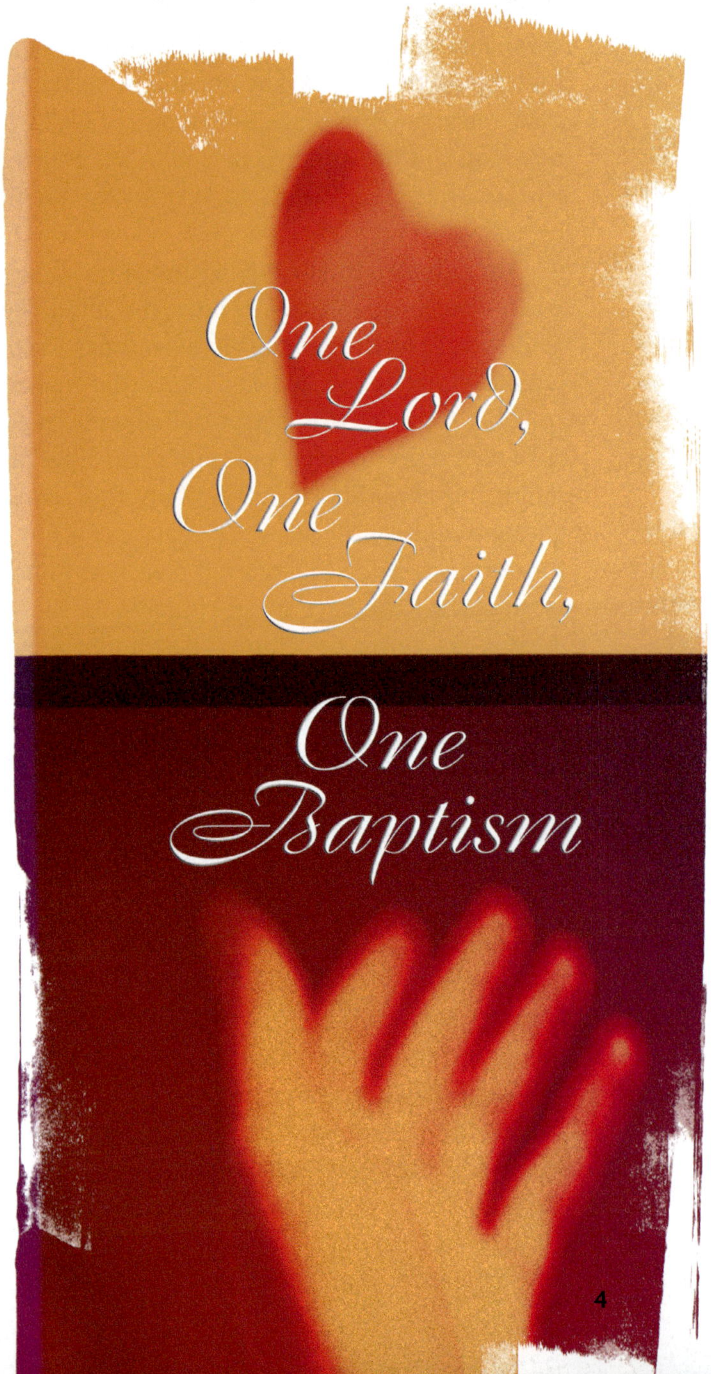


## History Repeating Itself

As you read this history of faith and salvation, recall the noteworthy words of Santayana: "Those who cannot remember the past are condemned to repeat it." Scripture is replete with reminders that the chosen nation of Israel consistently failed to remember its past. (See, for example, the impassioned speech in Acts 7.) And the Christian church is no less susceptible to the same failure.

We neglect the history of salvation to our own great peril. But we take great comfort in knowing that the God of history, the God of salvation, does not neglect us. He entered human history in human form, for us and for our salvation. And today, in history, through the proclamation of Christ, He is still working out the salvation of His people. You're one of them. Salvation history is your history. Acts is a chapter in your own story. ■

# Can I Get a Witness?

"Can I get a witness?" bellows a swaying preacher on a steamy southern Sunday. Early the next morning, a smartly dressed lawyer stands before a judge: "The defense calls its first witness, your honor." Later that afternoon, across town, a victim of schoolroom gossip protests in tears, "As God is my witness, I did not do that!"

In everyday speech we hear and use the word *witness* in a wide variety of ways. Some may be rhetorical and others technical, but all uses of the term have one very important aspect in common. Behind every call for a witness is a call for a reliable confirmation of the truth. It is no wonder then that Jesus, Himself "the way and the truth and the life" (John 14:6), should call and appoint men to act as His witnesses. The Acts of the Apostles consistently emphasizes that the Apostles serve as witnesses and their "acts" are examples of witnessing. Witnessing is the theme of Luke's history and it's the theme of the Christian life.

## Getting the Facts Straight

"You will be My witnesses," Jesus told His followers (Acts 1:8). But in what sense does He use this term? And in what sense does Luke use it as he records the story of this command being fulfilled? As noted above, calling for a witness is calling for confirmation of the truth. But what, specifically, is the truth Jesus wants the world to know about Him?

Remember the context in which Jesus spoke to His disciples. Luke tells us He spoke "after His suffering," that is, after His crucifixion and death, and after "He showed Himself to these men and gave many convincing proofs that He was alive" (Acts 1:3). Jesus was dead, but He rose from the dead. He had conquered death, the consequence of sin. And He gave His disciples convincing proofs of this fact. The apostle Peter explained: "He commanded us to preach to the people and to testify that He is the one whom God appointed as judge of the living and the dead" (Acts 10:42).

No doubt, some of the Jewish people who heard this testimony questioned whether it could be true. The title "judge of the living and dead" belongs to God alone (see Psalm 82:8 and Isaiah 66:16). Precisely! Jesus Himself claimed that "I and the Father are one" and that "anyone who has seen Me has seen the Father" (John 10:30 and 14:9). And then His claims to divinity were irrefutably proved by His resurrection from death. But who would believe such a thing had happened? Preposterous! Unless it could be confirmed by *eye*-witnesses.

That is exactly what the apostles were. "We are all witnesses of the fact," Peter says of the resurrection (Acts 2:32). And he says again later: "He was not seen by all the people, but by witnesses whom God had already chosen—by us who ate and drank with Him after He rose from the dead" (Acts 10:41). Even in choosing a replacement for Judas, the apostles were careful to pick one who had been with Jesus from His baptism until His ascension. The reason, they explained, was because he "must become a witness with us of His resurrection" (Acts 1:22). In matters of life and death—especially eternal life and death—an eyewitness is the one to trust for getting the facts straight. This is a point Peter makes most forcefully in his own writing: "We did not follow cleverly invented stories when we told you about the power and coming of our Lord Jesus Christ, but we were eyewitnesses of His majesty" (2 Peter 1:16).

## Getting the Facts Out

Witnesses, especially valuable eyewitnesses, are never simply left to keep the facts straight for themselves. They are called upon to get the facts out, to give testimony. And if the facts are as momentous as those of the Gospel story, they deserve more than a closed courtroom hearing. They deserve a hearing before the entire world. This Jesus

Living under Roman rule, the disciples would undoubtedly have been aware of the requirements placed on witnesses in an actual court of Roman law.

explicitly commanded: "This gospel of the kingdom will be preached *in the whole world* as a testimony to all nations" (Matthew 24:14). And again He told His disciples, "you will be My witnesses in Jerusalem, and in all Judea and Samaria, and *to the ends of the earth*" (Acts 1:8).

What a daunting task! Think about the butterflies that suddenly appear in your stomach as you work up the courage to invite one friend to church. Now ask what it would take to persuade you to knock at every door on the block, not only inviting the neighbors to church, but explaining the Gospel to them yourself (and, of course, telling them the uncomfortable truth that they are sinners in need of the Gospel). Do you even want to think about the heart it would take to then keep witnessing as you start walking—out of your neighborhood, into the next city, then on to the adjoining state, and even eventually into another country?

It wasn't an immediately appealing prospect to the apostles either. Remember where Jesus found them after His resurrection. Not out knocking on doors, but huddled in fear behind their own locked doors. Not only was serving as a witness a time-consuming and potentially humiliating task, it could even be fatal. Living under Roman rule, the disciples would undoubtedly have been aware of the requirements placed on witnesses in an actual court of Roman law. Before giving testimony one pledged one's home, property, and slaves, as well as freedom, family, and even one's own life. Were the testimony considered false, all would be lost. They had to put their money—and lives—where their mouths were. This was a serious matter in the ancient world. That is why Jesus did not leave His disciples to their own devices.

They would be sent out as witnesses, but only, Jesus said, after "the Holy Spirit comes on you" (Acts 1:8). They would not act or speak alone; the Spirit would work through them. From the very first He would be their guide, their encouragement, and their voice (see also Acts 4:8; 8:29; 13:4; 20:22). And by the Spirit's power, they said, "we cannot help speaking about what we have seen and heard" (Acts 4:20).

## Calling the Next Witness

Recall once again the words with which Jesus commissioned His disciples: "the Gospel ... will be preached," He said; "you will be My witnesses." Notice that it is not merely a request. It is not an option. His followers, even today, *will* be His witnesses. To continue the courtroom analogy, you have been subpoenaed. To reject the call is to be in contempt of court. And in a court where the Lord Himself is judge, that's a serious matter indeed.

Yes, giving testimony is still a time-consuming and potentially humiliating task. But it comes with a wonderfully comforting promise. "You will receive power when the Holy Spirit comes on you" (Acts 1:8). That power is yours already, having been given you in your Baptism. And the Holy Spirit, who dwells in you even now, Scripture assures, will "teach you at that time what you should say" (Luke 12:12). In fact, you already know the substance of it. Jesus Christ, who was crucified under Pontius Pilate, rose again on the third day. His death and resurrection purchased your salvation and that of the world. That's the truth. And like the apostles, we cannot help speaking about what we have heard. ■

# The Acts of Whom?

Maybe you've never been on the set of a movie. Maybe you've never watched a scene being filmed. But you know exactly how each scene begins—the director chants, "Lights! Camera! . . . Action!" With the drop of the clapboard arm, the actors begin to act. When the final production hits the theaters, that's all we see, actors acting. But of course we know that there was also a lot of action off-camera and behind the scenes: writers, directors, camera operators, and dozens more are necessary to make a movie.

Our modern fascination with actors and acting can sometimes lead us to forget that there are more people involved than those who confront us on the screen. It's hardly surprising, then, that we might be tempted to read the Book of Acts in the same manner. After all, the name *Acts* suggests acts, actors, and acting. But who exactly are the actors? Who's really doing the acting? The title "The Acts of the Apostles" provides one answer. The dramatic deeds of the apostles Peter, John, and Paul engage our attention throughout. But as with our contemporary Hollywood fare, incredibly significant work goes on behind the scenes: by Jesus Christ and the Holy Spirit.

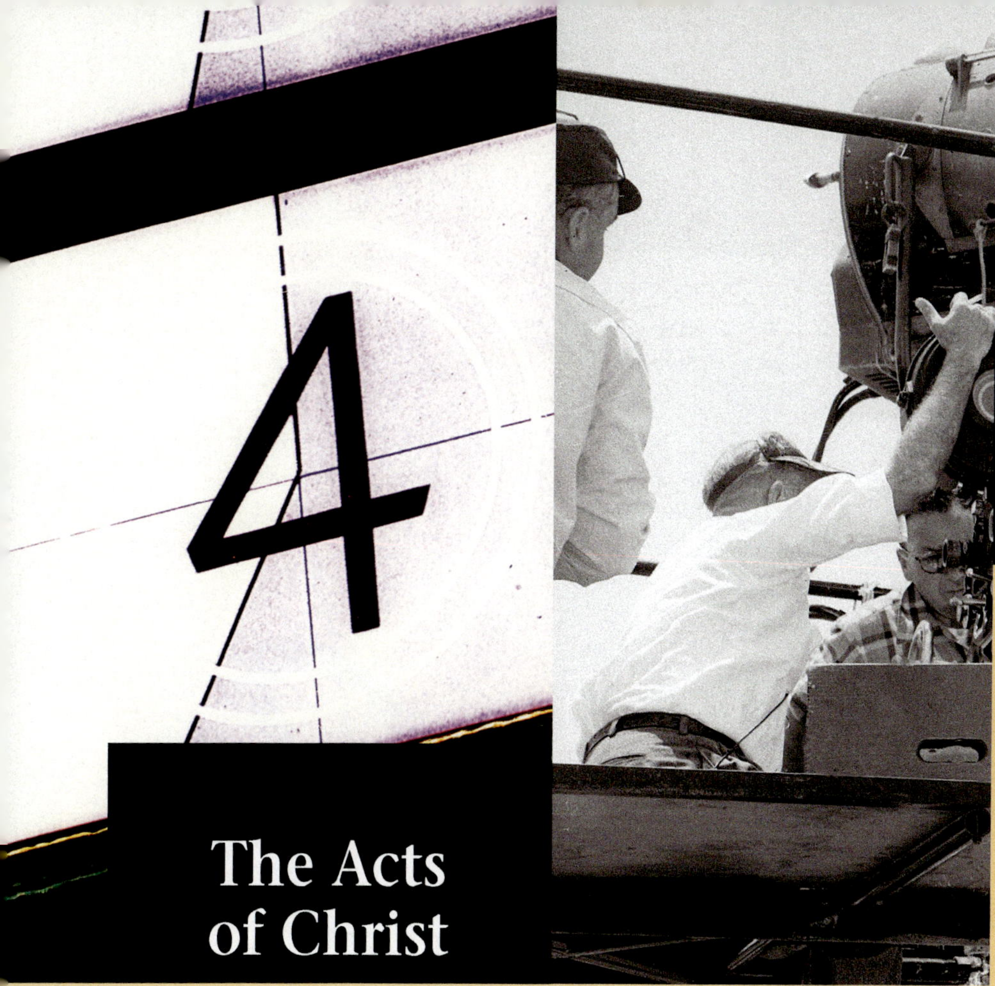

# 4 The Acts of Christ

Before His ascension, Jesus had given His disciples a promise: "I am with you always, to the very end of the age" (Matthew 28:20). Did they consider this statement nothing more than typical parting words, the same sort we might utter when telling friends we're "with them" in thought even though separated from them? Whatever the disciples may first have thought about Jesus' words, it soon became clear that He was with them in far more than a symbolic sense.

When Jewish authorities questioned Peter about the healing of a crippled beggar, for instance, Peter denied all responsibility. Instead, he said, "It is by the name of Jesus Christ . . . that this man stands before you healed" (Acts 4:10). It sounds strange, but makes sense; throughout His earthly life Jesus had indeed healed those brought before Him. In fact, all of the miraculous deeds performed by the disciples have their parallels in Jesus' own earthly ministry. Casting out demons? Jesus had been there. Raising the dead? Jesus had done that. Are these merely strange coincidences? Not at all!

Luke opens his history with a significant clue as to what's going on—and who's leading—in Acts. "In my former book," he notes, "I wrote about all that Jesus began to do and to teach" (Acts 1:1). The Gospel story is not simply an account of what Jesus did; it is the story of what He *began to do*. And its sequel records what Jesus *continued to do*. The risen Christ continues His ministry of salvation and restoration through the acts and works of His apostles. And the apostles, for their part, provide a stunning display of the truth behind St. Paul's statement: "I no longer live, but Christ lives in me" (Galatians 2:20).

## The Acts of the Spirit

Jesus, however, is not the only one living and acting in the lives of the apostles. He not only told them He would be with them, but He promised that His Spirit would likewise be with them (John 16:7). His presence is seen everywhere in Acts. In only 28 chapters Luke mentions the person of the Holy Spirit 57 times. And the apostles are fully aware of His presence. It is He who gave them the power to testify (Acts 1:8). The Spirit tells them where to testify (Acts 8:29). They stand up to testify "filled with the Holy Spirit" (Acts 4:8). And the Spirit Himself converts those hearing the proclamation of the Good News (Acts 10:44).

Make no mistake. The apostles serve as the Lord's instruments, but the Lord Himself is the one acting through them. As Luke outlines the growth of the church, he insists on one very fundamental point. This numerical growth is attributable to no human endeavors; rather, "the Lord added to their number" (Acts 2:47).

Ironically, a rather unlikely individual also seconds this most important point. When Gameliel, an unbelieving Pharisee, stood before the Sanhedrin he advised them: "Leave these men alone!

For if their purpose or activity is of human origin, it will fail. But if it is from God, you will not be able to stop these men" (Acts 5:38–39). The irony increases as we read his words two thousand years later. The activity of the disciples—or rather, of God Himself—has not failed! It continues even today as the Gospel is proclaimed and as the church continues to grow.

## Lights! Camera! Action!

What Luke, the apostles, and even Gameliel make so plain is, strangely enough, something we often tend to forget. The church grows where and when God Himself is at work. We are incredibly privileged; we, like the apostles, have been chosen to serve as His instruments. But we should never dare to think our acts alone are effective or sufficient in matters of salvation.

No matter how clever our programs or how eloquent our speech, if they do not bear witness to the salvation won by Christ we should not think the Spirit is using them to build up the kingdom of God. Many have been deceived by this notion. So-called Christian Science, Mormonism, and the Jehovah's Witnesses have grown at alarmingly rapid rates. Is this evidence of the work of Christ and His Spirit? Not at all! Jesus endowed His people with His Spirit that they might testify to Him, to His death and resurrection, and to the forgiveness of sins that He alone provides. Any preaching that does not do so can claim to flow neither from Christ nor His Spirit.

The sure promise given to the apostles is our promise yet today. Where Christ and His cross are preached, there Christ Himself is active. There His Spirit is present, calling, enlightening, and sanctifying His people. Each of us has been given a walk-on role in the divine drama of salvation, but the Lord Himself remains the actor with top billing. He acts in us, through us, and for us, even to the very end of the age. ■

| ACTION | HUMAN ACTOR | DIVINE ACTOR |
|---|---|---|
| Choosing an apostle to replace Judas (1:12–26) | The 11 apostles | The Lord: "Lord, You know everyone's heart. Show us which of these two You have chosen" (1:24). |
| Speaking in tongues (foreign languages) (2:1–21) | The 12 apostles | The Holy Spirit: "All of them were filled with the Holy Spirit and began to speak in other tongues as the Spirit enabled them" (2:4). |
| Healing a crippled beggar (3:1–4:10) | Peter | Jesus Christ: "In the name of Jesus Christ of Nazareth, walk" (3:6); "Why do you stare at us as if by our own power or godliness we had made this man walk?" (3:12); "It is Jesus' name and the faith that comes through Him that has given this complete healing to him" (3:16); "It is by the name of Jesus Christ of Nazareth, whom you crucified but whom God raised from the dead, that this man stands before you healed" (4:10). |
| Speaking God's Word boldly (4:29–31) | Peter, John, and the believers | The Lord: "Now, Lord, consider their threats and enable your servants to speak Your word with great boldness" (4:29). The Spirit: "And they were all filled with the Holy Spirit and spoke the word of God boldly" (4:31). |
| Increasing the numbers of believers | The apostles and other disciples | The Lord: "And the Lord added to their number daily those who were being saved" (2:47); "The Lord's hand was with them, and a great number of people believed and turned to the Lord" (11:21). God: "If their purpose or activity is of human origin, it will fail. But if it is from God, you will not be able to stop these men; you will only find yourselves fighting against God" (5:38–39). The Spirit: "The church ... was strengthened; and encouraged by the Holy Spirit, it grew in numbers" (9:31). |
| Speaking wisely (6:8–7:53) | Stephen | The Spirit: "These men began to argue with Stephen, but they could not stand up against his wisdom or the Spirit by whom he spoke" (6:9–10). |
| Bestowing the Holy Spirit (8:9–24) | Peter and John: "Peter and John placed their hands on them, and they received the Holy Spirit" (8:17) | God: Peter calls this ability "the gift of God" (8:20). |
| Deciding where to evangelize (8:26–40) | Philip | The Spirit: "The Spirit told Philip, 'Go to that chariot and stay near it'" (8:29); "When they came up out of the water, the Spirit of the Lord suddenly took Philip away" (8:39). |
| Healing the paralytic Aeneas (9:32–35) | Peter | Jesus Christ: "'Aeneas,' Peter said to him, 'Jesus Christ heals you'" (9:34). |

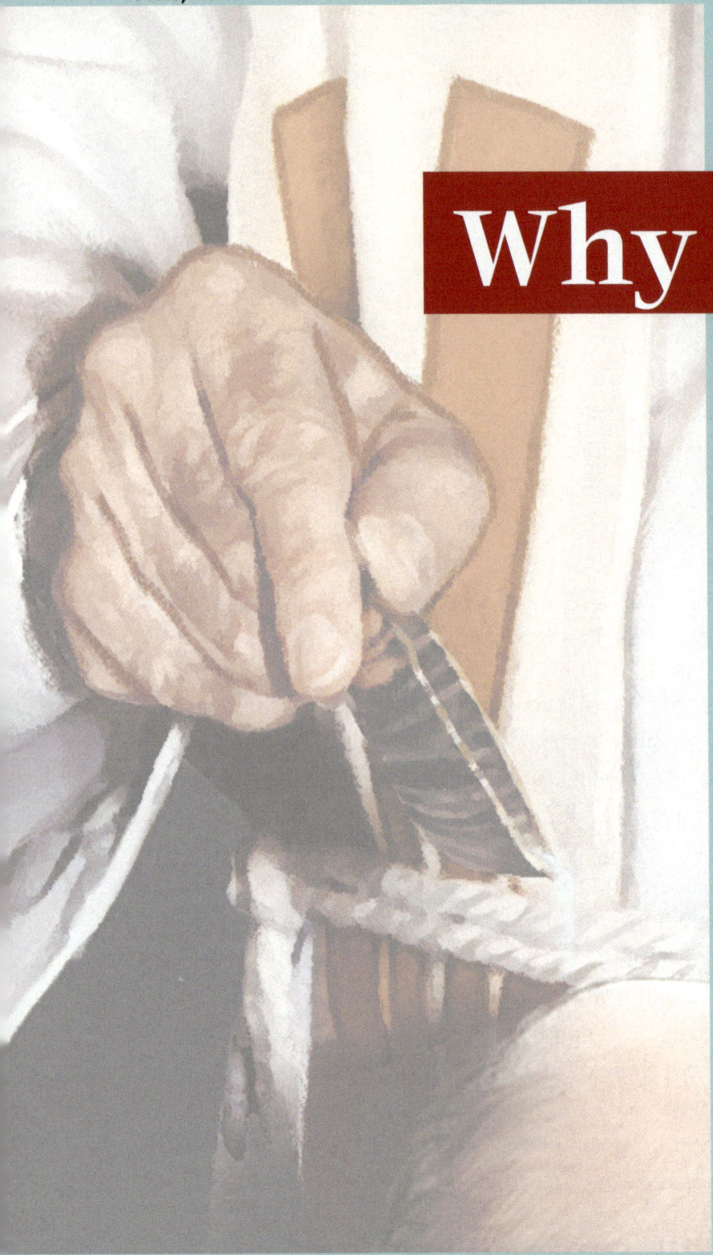

# Why Shouldn't I?

The Ethiopian eunuch whom Philip met on the road between Jerusalem and Gaza illustrates an exemplary response to God's gracious gifts (Acts 8:26–40). As he heard the Good News about Jesus, the man silently pondered the message of salvation. As the Holy Spirit worked in him, he humbly asked Philip, "Why shouldn't I be baptized?" Note: he did not ask, "Why *should* I be baptized?" but "Why *shouldn't* I?" In other words, why should I not let God wash away my sins with simple water and word?

How different is the eunuch's question from that which we often hear! So often we hear—or perhaps even ask—why should I be baptized? Or why should I baptize my children? To these questions one could add: why should I go to church? receive the Lord's Supper? read the Bible? After all, the self-justification runs, it's not *absolutely* necessary. The thief on the cross beside Jesus is brought forward as an inevitable example. He had no time for Baptism. Yet Jesus promised him "today you will be with Me in paradise" (Luke 23:43). If I have faith, surely God will receive me without Baptism, church, and the Lord's Supper. Why should they inconvenience me?

## The Divine Mandate

These questions may be called "Law" questions. That is, they search for some hard-and-fast rule in answer. Scripture does provide such an answer. Why should you baptize your children or be baptized yourself? Because it is a divine mandate. It is a command spoken by God Himself. Before Jesus ascended into heaven, He told His apostles to go and make disciples. How exactly? By "baptizing them in the name of the Father and of the Son and of the Holy Spirit" (Matthew 28:19).

Asking a Law question begs for a Law answer. And God's Law is irrefutable. But the Law does not provide the only answer. In fact, it does not even provide the best answer. The best answer is one based on the Gospel. The best answer comes not in response to the Law question "Why should I?" but in response to the Gospel question "Why shouldn't I?"

Jesus' message is clear. Disciples are made in the water and words of Baptism. Those who would be disciples are those who would be baptized. And Jesus' mandate was something His apostles accepted with utmost seriousness. When Peter's Pentecost audience asked their own "Law" question—"what shall we do?"—the apostle immediately replied, "Repent and be baptized, every one of you" (Acts 2:37–38). Peter showed his seriousness again in the house of Cornelius, where he "ordered that they be baptized in the name of Jesus Christ" (Acts 10:48).

## The Divine Promise

When the Ethiopian eunuch asked Philip, "Why shouldn't I?" it was in response to what he had heard. Philip had "told him the good news about Jesus" (Acts 8:35). Philip had told him the Gospel of Jesus' death and resurrection. In short, Philip had told him about God's greatest gift: the forgiveness of sins. And the Ethiopian's reply was nothing other than the willingness to receive this gift. As Peter had preached at Pentecost, Baptism in God's threefold name bestows this gift; it is "for the forgiveness of your sins" (Acts 2:38). And, as he would later write in his first epistle, Baptism "now saves you" (1 Peter 3:21).

The question of the Ethiopian eunuch was not a request for a law. It was a request for the Gospel. In response to Philip's clear proclamation of divine forgiveness, he essentially asked, "Why should I not receive this forgiveness? It is, after all, what God wishes me to have. It is what He sent His only Son to procure for me. Why should I not allow Him to do as He pleases, to be gracious to me?"

## Look, Here Is Water

Think for a moment about how you respond to those offering you gifts. When presented with a token of someone's love for you do you respond by asking, "Why should I have to accept this?" Do you go further still and actually reject the gift? No, not at all! To do so would be extremely rude. In fact, rejecting such a gift could quite rightly be interpreted as a rejection of the one giving it.

How much more offensive would it be to reject a gift offered by our Lord Himself? He possesses the greatest gift of all: eternal salvation. And it was purchased at immense cost, the price being the life of His own Son. But He did not think that too high a price to pay for those He loves. He loves you. And because He so loves you He greatly desires to shower you with His good gifts: forgiveness, life, and salvation. In the sacrament of Baptism God freely offers these gracious gifts. "Look, here is water," the Ethiopian eunuch responded, "Why shouldn't I?" No greater question can be asked even today. ■

USED BY PERMISSION FROM ISRAEL MINISTRY OF TOURISM

**Neither the rough terrain of Judea nor the rough treatment from its citizens prevented the prosperity of the Gospel. The disciples "preached the word wherever they went" (Acts 8:4).**

# Persecution and Prosperity

**The onward march of the Christian church is Luke's consistent theme.** To make sure that we don't miss this theme, Luke stops occasionally to remind us. He pauses once to note that "the word of God spread" and that "the number of disciples in Jerusalem increased rapidly" (Acts 6:7). A few chapters later he again tells us that "the church throughout Judea, Galilee and Samaria . . . grew in numbers" (Acts 9:31). And just in case we'd forgotten, he can't resist the reminder that "the word of God continued to increase and spread" (Acts 12:24). Twice more (in Acts 16:5 and 19:20) he reiterates the same theme.

Notice something else about these reminders. Each alternates between mention of "the church" and "the word of God." This is surely no accident. Why does the church grow? Because it proclaims God's Word! And in doing so, it allows God Himself to act. That He does so effectively, not only protecting but also strengthening and increasing His church through His Word, provides ample "evidence of the grace of God" (Acts 11:23).

## Wine and Roses?

Though God is ever present and active, Luke has also made it abundantly clear that life in the Christian church is not all wine and roses. It wasn't in the first century, and it certainly won't be in the twenty-first. Acts offers us a timely warning about thinking otherwise. Contemporary preachers proclaiming a gospel of health and wealth are not proclaiming the Gospel we find preached in Acts. The Christian and apostolic Gospel is the promise of forgiveness. Luke makes no promises of health or wealth; he reminds us instead that we could very well face poverty and persecution. He makes no promise—as some books found in Christian bookstores do—that believers will have idyllic marriages and angelic children. Sin and its consequences will never cease to beset our families and our churches.

Though we have been left with no promise of wine and roses, we have been left with something infinitely more beneficial: wine and bread. And likewise, water and Word. These do indeed come with God's own promise. And what a wonderful promise it is, the promise of the very Gospel itself. Here you receive the means by which the church has always grown and been strengthened. As you received the waters of Baptism, you became part of the church's history. As you partake of Christ's body and blood in the bread and wine, your faith is strengthened so that you, too, might carry on the church's mission. You are strengthened to proclaim God's saving Word to those who will become actors in the next chapter of the church's history. Wine, water, and Word. Common, ordinary, and everyday. Through such things God acted in the church of Acts, and through such things He continues to work today. ■

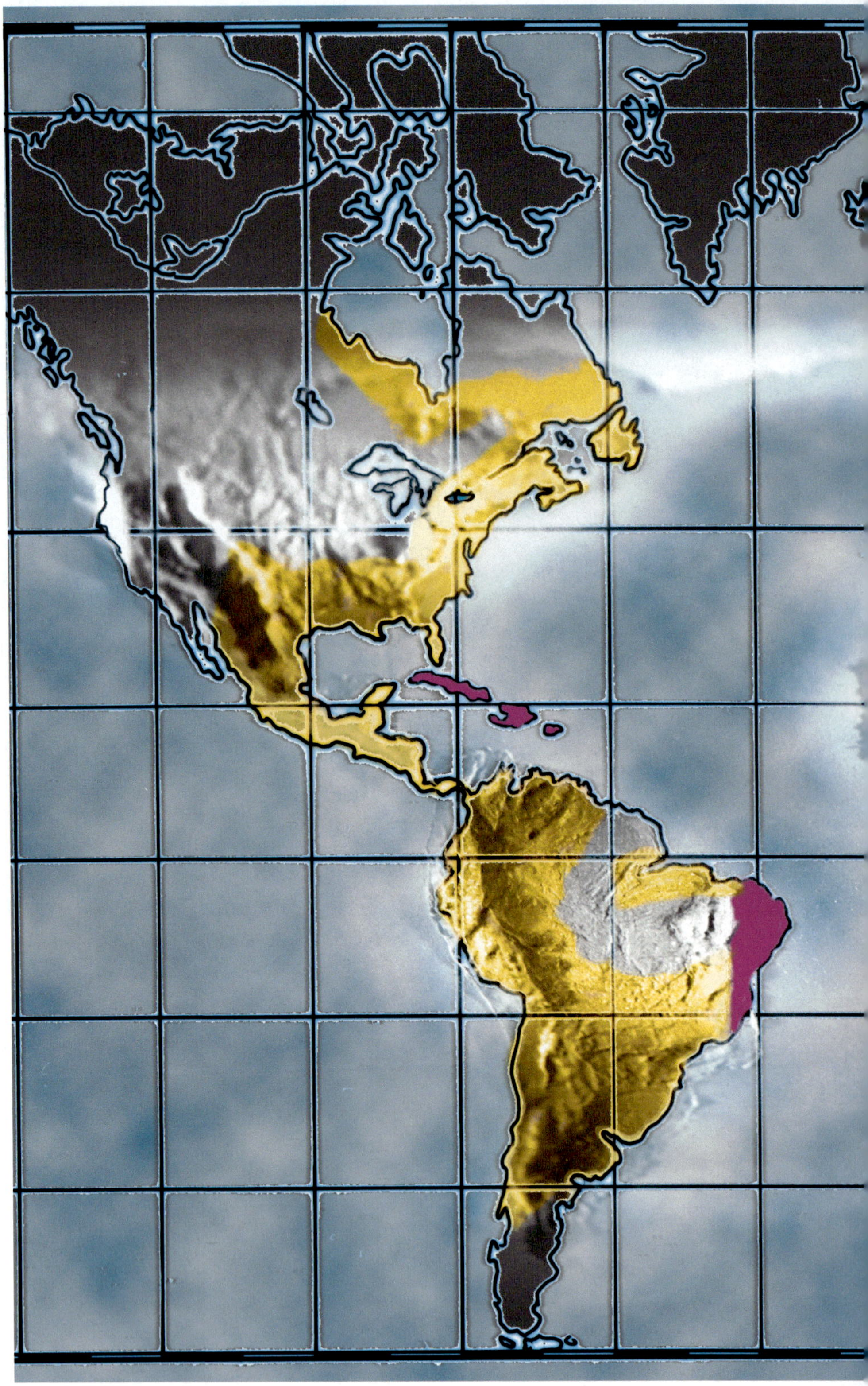

**The Spread of Chrisitanity**

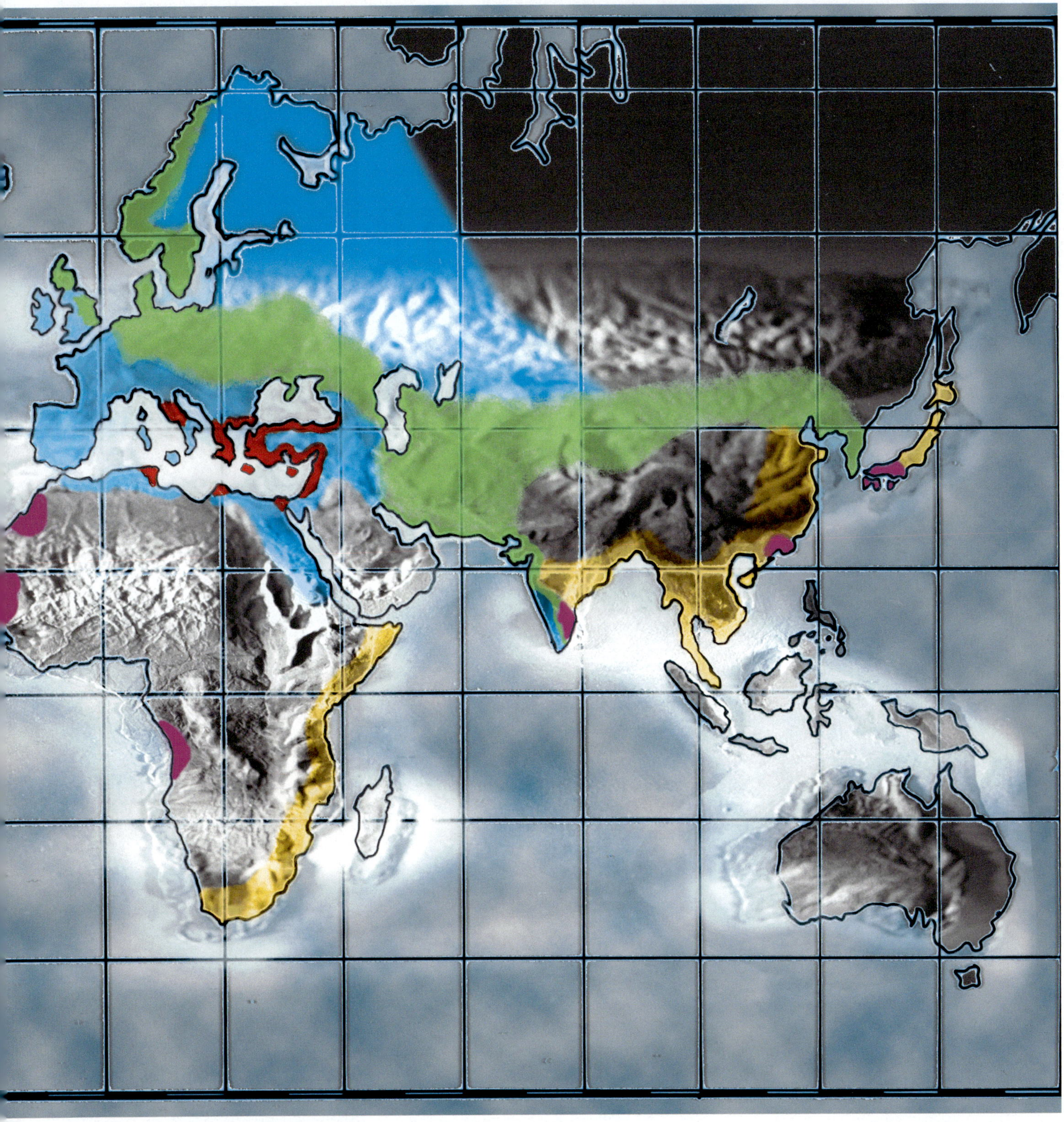

**Red—100 A.D.** **Green—1100 A.D.** **Yellow—1800 A.D.**
**Blue—400 A.D.** **Violet—1600 A.D.** **Grey—2000 A.D.**

# THE SCANDAL OF THE ORDINARY

***Four-year-olds bounce from couch to coffee table, imagining themselves superheroes. Many students distinguish themselves with tattoos, piercings, and brightly colored hair. Married couples don't just wonder how to keep up with the Joneses, they seek to surpass them along with the Smiths and the Taylors and the rest. Senior citizens swap stories about unusual medical conditions. People long to avoid the dreaded label of "ordinary." Who wants to be "plain Jane" or "average Joe"? Strangely, the most extraordinary person of all: the Son of God.***

## The Undynamic Duo

We have no way of knowing what Peter and John may have hoped to become when they grew up. Certainly not apostles. Certainly not wandering preachers who would face ridicule, rejection, and persecution. True, it was not at all an ordinary vocation. In fact, compared to their previous employment as fishermen, it was quite extraordinary. But, of course, they didn't go seeking this job. Their employer went seeking them. Jesus, walking one day along the Sea of Galilee, personally handpicked them to be His disciples (see Mark 1:14–20).

Uneducated and inarticulate men with no previous experience—and smelling more than faintly of fish—that's who the Son of God chose to represent Him. Marketers, personnel directors, and human-resource coordinators would surely second-guess Jesus' peculiar emploment policies. And they would not be alone. The people of the first century were equally confused. "When they saw the courage of Peter and John and realized that they were unschooled, ordinary men, they were astonished" (Acts 4:13). Was this astonishment simply an overreaction? Was there something extraordinary about Peter and John that they'd missed?

## Unschooled, Ordinary Men

Peter was eager to prove that Jesus had not made a mistake in calling him to be a disciple. He was determined to prove that he was no ordinary fisherman. Having laid up his boat and nets, he would be the best "fisher of men" his Lord could hope for. When Jesus asked His disciples who they believed Him to be, Peter was quick to answer: "You are the Christ" (Mark 8:29). And it was Peter, full of confidence, who jumped out of a boat to imitate his Lord walking on the water (Matthew 14:22–31). When Peter began to sink, it must have dawned on him that he was pretty ordinary after all.

But this didn't discourage Peter for long. When Jesus informed His disciples that they would fall away, proud Peter scoffed: "Even if all fall away, I will not" (Mark 14:29). And if words were not proof enough, he had a sword to make his point more emphatically. When guards seized Christ in Gethsemane, Peter quickly entered the fray and severed a man's ear (John 18:10).

How strange, then, were the actions of this extraordinarily zealous disciple only a few hours later. While Jesus stood before the Sanhedrin, Peter sat in the courtyard below. And there he not only denied being Jesus' preeminent disciple; he denied knowing the man at all

(Mark 14:66–72)—not once, not twice, but three times. Then he wept in shame. In that experience Peter realized that he was all too ordinary indeed: cowardly, selfish, and sinful. Maybe, he thought, it was time to return to his old, average life. "I'm going out to fish," he soon said (John 21:3). Back to fishing! After all he had seen and heard of Jesus!

The apostle John also had high hopes of rising above the average and the mundane. Peter may have shown himself to be the chief disciple during Jesus' earthly ministry, but there was still heaven to look forward to. So one day John, along with his brother James, marched up to Jesus and asked for no ordinary favor. "Let one of us sit at Your right and the other at Your left in Your glory" (Mark 10:37; Matthew 20:20–23 reveals that it was John's mother who made the request on her son's behalf). Though the request was denied, John remained determined to show himself worthy of the position. When some Samaritans rejected Jesus, John volunteered to summon fire from heaven to destroy them (Luke 9:54). No less than Peter, he took an extraordinarily forceful view of defending Jesus' honor!

But also like Peter, John showed himself to be an ordinary, fellow sinner. When Jesus asked him to remain awake in prayer, he nodded off repeatedly (Mark 14:32–42). With the rest of the disciples, he hid in fear after Jesus' death. And he was rebuked with them for his lack of faith (Mark 16:14). Neither John nor Peter—nor any of the apostles—was a "great man" by human standards. They, like each of us, shared the common traits of fallen humanity. They could be petty and selfish, rash and unthoughtful, proud and faithless. In short, they were sinful. They were ordinary.

## Scandalous Indeed

After the apostles spent time with Jesus, their ordinary appearance scandalized those who met them. Those who heard and saw them were "astonished" (Acts 4:13) and filled with "wonder and amazement" (Acts 3:10). How could such extraordinary things be done by such ordinary men? How could such an undynamic duo do such dynamic deeds? The answer, of course, is that these were not human deeds at all. They were the very acts of God. At Pentecost the disciples had received the power of the Holy Spirit as promised by Jesus (Acts 1:8; here the Greek word for "power" is *dunamis,* from which we get the word *dynamite*). God Himself acted through these ordinary, unschooled men even as He continues to act through ordinary, unspectacular means today.

God's dealings with the ordinary continue to scandalize. Especially when we show that we ourselves are no more than ordinary. Like Peter and John, we're tempted to think that we can, even must, earn God's favor. Perhaps not by means so dramatic as swords in our hands or demands for fire on our lips, but in ways equally misguided. We're tempted to trumpet our good works and congratulate ourselves on what we consider extraordinary piety. And we're sorely offended by the reminder that "all our righteous acts are like filthy rags" (Isaiah 64:6). The scandalous fact is that, by our own reason and strength, we cannot lift ourselves above our ordinary, sinful status. And attempts to do so result in failures just as shameful as those of Peter and John.

Thank goodness, God knows full well that we are unable to raise ourselves out of sin. Therefore, He lowered Himself into our place. He became what we are: He became sin so that sin might be conquered (2 Corinthians 5:21). For our salvation, Jesus took on ordinary human flesh and died the death of a common, ordinary man. This is what St. Paul calls truly *scandalous* (a Greek word meaning "that which causes offense"). The scandal is God Himself on a cross (1 Corinthians 1:23). Yet this is the very Gospel.

God's way with us has not changed even today. He still brings salvation by means of the common and the ordinary. He calls ordinary, sinful people to proclaim His forgiveness. He clothes Himself in the common elements of bread and wine to feed us and our faith. And under the form of ordinary water, He puts His name upon us and calls us His children. We can hope for nothing more extraordinary than that precious title. ■

© IMAGE SOURCE/SUPERSTOCK

# Preaching Christ and His Cross

Though pastors may not like to admit it, their congregations often have humorous ways of describing their sermons. They may speak of "show-and-tell" sermons (using a prop to make a point). "Groaners" are full of bad puns or jokes. And we've all heard "skyscraper" sermons: one story after another. Different styles suit different preachers and different parishes.

Regardless of style, the subject of Christian preaching will always remain the same. Whether in the first century or the twenty-first, Christ and His cross are central to the Christian proclamation of forgiveness.

## Word and Spirit

That Christian preaching, despite many variations, should have a consistency from congregation to congregation and even from age to age will not come as a complete surprise. Christian pastors, after all, preach from the same holy Scripture. In liturgical churches, which make use of regular Bible readings, preachers use the same texts on a given Sunday. But they also have something even more profound in common, what St. Paul calls the "unity of the Spirit" (Ephesians 4:3). Jesus told the first band of preachers, "it will not be you speaking, but the Spirit of your Father speaking through you" (Matthew 10:20).

> *He suffered for you, for your iniquity*

As Jesus later explained in the Book of Acts, this is a primary reason why the Spirit has been given. He provides those who proclaim Christ with the power and the words to do so. This was certainly the case with the apostles. Luke notes, for example, that Peter spoke "filled with the Holy Spirit," as later also did Paul (Acts 4:8; 13:9). They, like the prophets before them, "spoke from God as they were carried along by the Holy Spirit" (2 Peter 1:21).

And this Spirit is not absent in the preaching of Christian pastors, those who today inhabit the apostolic office and carry on the apostolic mission. This is not to say that those who enter the pulpit in your local congregation are somehow "possessed" by the Spirit or speaking against their will. Nor is it an excuse for preachers to neglect the proper preparation of sermons. God called them and the church ordained them to proclaim the Word. And to do so one must be immersed in the Word. In fact, it is through this God-breathed Word of Scripture that the Spirit works in them, through their speech, and finally in the heart of you, the listener.

Not only is the written Word preached, but more specifically, pastors are called to preach the incarnate Word. "The Word became flesh," John wrote of Jesus in his Gospel (1:14). And it is this divine Word who told His first preachers that "you will be *My* witnesses" (Acts 1:8). Speeches that do not witness to Christ, the divine Word, may offer fine principles for moral living. They may be moving, uplifting, and encouraging. But if Jesus is not proclaimed they remain no more than speeches. They are not, properly speaking, Christian sermons.

## The Pattern of Preaching

Unfortunately, even with a firm emphasis on Christ it is entirely possible to preach something other than Christianity. Some portray Jesus as a new law-giver, like Moses (resulting in preaching that sounds more Judaic than Christian). Others hold Jesus up simply as a moral example (resulting in ethical philosophy rather than Christian theology). These messages, sadly, miss the central fact of the Christian message. So what does truly inspired Christian preaching look like? Well, let's see.

The first apostolic sermon was preached by Peter at Pentecost (Acts 2:14–36). He immediately turned the attention of his audience to Jesus. He boldly announced, "you, with the help of wicked men, put Him to death by nailing Him to the cross." It's a crushing condemnation of their sin. But he immediately proclaims: "But God raised Him from the dead." What does this mean? Peter continues: This means that Jesus is "both Lord and Christ." That grabbed their attention! So how does he conclude? "Repent and be baptized, every one of you, in the name of Jesus Christ for the forgiveness of your sins. And you will receive the gift of the Holy Spirit."

From condemnation to forgiveness, from crushing Law to comforting Gospel—this is the divine pattern of Christian preaching. And it is seen again and again in the Book of Acts (see chart on pp. 24–25). Christ was put to death on account of human sin, but raised again by the power of God. Repentance is needed and forgiveness is extended. This is the core of the Christian message: the reality of human guilt, but the greater reality of God's gift.

It may not be fancy, but this unadulterated preaching of Law and Gospel, of sin and salvation, is certainly effective. Through it the Holy Spirit brought thousands of believers into the faith in only a few short years. And it's through this preaching that millions of sinners are saved yet today. Nothing less will do. The great preacher St. Paul said bluntly, "If Christ has not been raised, our preaching is useless" (1 Corinthians 15:14). He might also have gone further: if we do not *announce* that Christ has been raised, our preaching is useless. So that announcement has been the hallmark of pure Christian preaching from the apostolic age to our own. Our sin resulted in His death, but His resurrection results in our salvation.

## We Are Here to Listen

The message of the apostle Peter, and of all Christian preachers, is universal; it applies to us all. Yes, Peter's Pentecost sermon was preached to a particular audience in a particular place at a particular time. But its truth has not changed, even the uncomfortable truth that Peter announced, "You, with the help of wicked men, put Him to death" (Acts 2:23). Resist the temptation to read that statement as a condemnation of his original Jewish audience alone. Your sin, no less than their nails, held Jesus to the cross. He suffered for you, for your iniquity. That is hard truth to hear. Yet a faithful preacher will not neglect to proclaim it.

But neither will he neglect to proclaim the joyous promise that follows. God raised Jesus up for your salvation. He has removed your sin and its terrible consequences. He grants you now His Holy Spirit, the gift given in your Baptism. These are Christ's promises. And they are the promises that He has entrusted to all those He continues to call and appoint to preach His holy Word. Trusting that they will faithfully proclaim these promises to us, we can say with those who once heard Peter proclaim them: "Now we are all here in the presence of God to listen to everything the Lord has commanded you to tell us" (Acts 10:33). ■

# Pattern of Christian

| TOPICS COVERED / SERMON | PROPHECY HAS BEEN FULFILLED | THE TESTIMONY OF MIRACLES | JESUS WAS CRUCIFIED | JESUS WAS RAISED |
|---|---|---|---|---|
| PETER ON PENTECOST (2:14–39) | vv. 16–21 Gift of the Spirit | v. 22 Accredited by God | v. 23 Nailed to the Cross | vv. 24–32 Freed from agony of death |
| PETER AT THE TEMPLE (3:12–26) | vv. 18, 22–24 Suffering Prophet | v. 12 God glorified Jesus | vv. 13–15 You disowned the Holy One | v. 15 God raised Him |
| PETER BEFORE THE SANHEDRIN (4:8–12) | v. 11 Chrsit the Capstone | v. 9 Crippled man healed by Crist | v. 10 You crucified Christ | v. 10 God raised Him |
| PETER BEFORE THE SANHEDRIN (5:29–32) | | | v. 30 Hung on a tree | v. 30 God raised Him |
| PETER AT HOUSE OF CORNELIUS (10:34–48) | v. 43 Faith and forgiveness | vv. 37–38 Anointed to do good | v. 39 Hung on a tree | v. 40 God raised Him |

# Preaching

| These things were witnessed | Jesus is the Christ [Savior] | Repentance is necessary | Forgiveness/ salvation is offered | The Spirit is given to believers | Baptism is response |
|---|---|---|---|---|---|
| v. 32<br>Witnesses of the resurrection | v. 36<br>Made Lord and Christ | v. 38<br>Repent and be baptized | v. 38<br>Forgiveness through Baptism | v. 38<br>Spirit given through Baptism | v. 38<br>Baptized in the name of Jesus Christ |
| v. 15<br>Witnesses of the resurrection | v. 20<br>The appointed Christ | v. 26<br>Turn from wicked ways | vv. 19, 26<br>Sins wiped out | | |
| | v. 12<br>Salvation in no one else | | v. 12<br>Saved by His name | | |
| v. 32<br>We and the Spirit are witnesses | v. 31<br>Exalted as Prince and Savior | v. 31<br>God gives repentance | v. 31<br>God gives forgiveness to Israel | | v. 32<br>God gives the Spirit |
| vv. 39, 41<br>Witnesses chosen by God | v. 36<br>Good news of peace | | v. 43<br>Forgiveness through His name | vv. 44–46<br>Spirit given to Gentiles | vv. 47–48<br>Baptized in the name of Jesus |

# GRACE, POWER & MARTYRDOM

A pirouetting ballerina is graceful; a charging bull is powerful. Butterflies are graceful; B-52s are powerful. We don't often think of the terms "grace" and "power" together. To refer to a martyr as full of "grace and power," as Stephen is described in Acts 6:8, may seem strange. A martyr is powerless; a victim of those who hold the power of life and death. Also, martyrdom is far from a graceful affair. Bones are crushed under a rain of stones, limbs are severed between the teeth of Colosseum lions, flesh melts in the heat of a blazing fire. It's all more gruesome than graceful.

In the Book of Acts, there is more to martyrdom than may at first be apparent. The Greek word *martyr* means, literally, "witness." That is precisely what Stephen was, even before his death. It was in fact his testimony to God's grace that precipitated his death. And when he preached *grace* he did so with *power*. Luke describes him as "a man full of faith and of the Holy Spirit" (Acts 6:5). And Jesus had promised His followers, "you will receive power when the Holy Spirit comes on you" (Acts 1:8). Witnessing to God's grace, and witnessing by God's power. In the person of Stephen—and in all witnesses and martyrs of the church—we see this central theme of Acts.

## Witnesses True and False

As the events of Stephen's death make clear, all witnesses are not equal. When Stephen gave testimony of Christ by the power of the Holy Spirit, the human wisdom of his opponents could not refute him. So, Luke tells us, "they produced false witnesses" (Acts 6:13). They falsely charged that Stephen had blasphemed against God and His prophets and rejected the divine Law of Israel. But as Stephen narrated to them the history of Israel, it quickly became evident that his accusers were the ones guilty of rejecting God's Law and prophets. Stephen's testimony exposed them. So they killed him.

The sham trial of Stephen bears remarkable similarity to that of His Lord. As Christ stood before Caiaphas, "the chief priests and the whole Sanhedrin were looking for false evidence against Jesus so that they could put Him to death. But they did not find any, though many false witnesses came forward" (Matthew 26:59–60). When Jesus finally opened His mouth to confess truthfully that He was the Son of God, He was promptly charged with blasphemy and sentenced to death.

Just as false witnesses are found throughout Scripture, so false martyrs abound even today. Kamikaze pilots in World War II, suicide bombers in the Middle East, imprisoned terrorists starving on hunger strikes. We are often led to believe that all who die in the name of a cause—even when wrong or misguided—deserve a certain amount of respect for the strength of their convictions. Many would argue that they at least deserve a headline. They are, we are told, martyrs. However, we do well to recall the sentiment of the early Christians. Death does not make a martyr, they would agree, but the content of one's testimony while still alive does.

## The Seed of the Church

The early Christian writer Tertullian (c. 160–c. 225) asserted, "The blood of Christians is seed" (*Apology*, chapter 50). Through the spectacle of martyrdom, he meant, the church gained victory over those who would destroy it. The patient suffering of Christians inspired more people to follow Christ. However, other Christian writers recorded stories of zealous but confused believers who went to great lengths to seek out martyrdom. For example, the mother of a young man named Origen was forced to hide his clothing in order to prevent him from leaving the house in search of a martyr's death.

But Scripture is clear. The death of sinners—even the death of those who are also saints—is not the foundation on which the church is built. The church is built on one foundation: Jesus Christ. Only the proclamation of His death and its saving benefits is responsible for the church's growth on earth. And only those who by the Spirit's power proclaim God's grace in Christ are truly His witnesses, or martyrs. This is so even if they do not meet death for their faithful testimony.

The above-mentioned Origen, who went on to become one of

the most influential theologians of the early church, finally realized this truth. "Everyone," he later wrote, "who bears witness to the truth [of Christianity], whether he supports it by words or deeds, in whatever way, may properly be called a martyr."

But you, like the witnesses and martyrs of the earliest church, have not been left to your own power. In the waters of Baptism God bestowed upon you His own grace and His own power. Like Stephen, even you are "full of God's grace and power." By His grace you are saved. And by His power you can now testify to the salvation He has provided for all. This in fact is precisely what you have been called to do. This is what the Holy Spirit has empowered you to do. You are to be a witness. You are to be, in the original meaning of the term, a martyr.

You may not, as Stephen did, see heaven open as you fall under a hail of stones. And that's probably good news. But what is certainly good news is that you will indeed see heaven open when you depart this earthly life. And there you will see the Savior in all His power and glory, graciously welcoming you home. ■

## Seeing Heaven Open

The chances are very slim that you will experience the dramatic death associated with martyrdom. But you certainly cannot expect to escape death itself. Death entered our world on account of sin. St. Paul reminds us "in this way death came to all men, because all sinned" (Romans 5:12). The fact of your mortality is a constant reminder that you are a sinful being living in a sinful world. And nothing within your power can change that.

# A Strange Instrument

"If you can't fix it, get a bigger hammer." This well-worn joke illustrates the frustration commonly caused by tools. As with many jokes, the humor is in the absurdity. Nobody gaps spark plugs or adjusts an engine's idle with a hammer. But we've probably all found ourselves, at one time or another, in a situation where we've had to use a less-than-appropriate tool. Perhaps it was turning screws with a butter knife or pounding tacks with a shoe heel. Or maybe, in desperation, putting our teeth into service as makeshift pliers.

© CHUCK SAVAGE/CORBIS

God, in contrast, is all-knowing and all-powerful. He need not worry about finding Himself in such awkward situations. He always chooses the most logical instrument to carry out His plans, right? A brief read through Acts might lead us to question this assertion. In fact, the testimony of Scripture from Genesis forward compels us to rethink our definition of what "logical" means to the mind of God. For example, the hundred-year-old Sarah surely wasn't the most logical choice to give birth to the nation of Israel. A humble, unknown virgin named Mary certainly wasn't the most logical choice to give birth to the world's Savior. And Saul? He appears the most illogical instrument of all.

## A Pharisee, the Son of a Pharisee

When Saul, by this time renamed Paul, stood before the Sanhedrin, he introduced himself as "a Pharisee, the son of a Pharisee" (Acts 23:6). By these words he meant to emphasize his association with that strict sect of Judaism. Though we know them as Pharisees, they often referred to themselves as *chasidim*, or "pious ones." As the name suggests, and as the Gospel authors affirm, they were zealously legalistic, not only with regard to the Bible, but also regarding manmade rules and rituals. The Pharisees, like many religious sects today, gave equal weight to the words of Scripture and the sayings of their teachers. Thus the Pharisees were the ones who constantly harangued Jesus for His disregard for the traditions of the elders.

Saul was no exception to this pharisaical legalism. Rather, he was its epitome. Calling himself "a Pharisee, the son of a Pharisee" was something of an understatement. He had in fact been educated under the great Gamaliel, one of the most respected Jewish teachers of his day. And Paul himself admitted that he had been so zealous for the laws of his people that he had "persecuted the followers of this Way [Christianity] to their death, arresting both men and women and throwing them into prison" (see Acts 22:3–5).

This, Luke informs us, was decidedly not an understatement. Saul was not only present to supervise the stoning of the Christian Stephen; he was there "giving approval to his death" (Acts 8:1). That day, Luke continues, "a great persecution broke out against the church." And at its forefront was none other than Saul, "still breathing out murderous threats against the Lord's disciples" (Acts 9:1). But, as he would soon learn, he was not merely persecuting the church and the disciples.

Violently and mysteriously thrown to the ground on his way to Damascus, he heard an unknown voice calling his name. When he asked who spoke,

the answer was shocking: "I am Jesus, whom you are persecuting" (Acts 9:5).

## God's Chosen Instrument

Pharisaical legalist. Church enemy. Murderer of Stephen. Persecutor of Christ. A more unlikely and illogical instrument for the spread of Christianity could hardly be found. And yet the same Lord who spoke to Saul on the road to Damascus soon told Ananias that "this man is My chosen instrument" (Acts 9:15). It's utterly astounding! But even more

THE CONVERSION OF ST. PAUL, © CHRISTIE'S / SUPERSTOCK

strange is that the Lord stated that Saul is to be His instrument "to carry My name before the Gentiles." Not only to the Jews, whose laws and customs he knew so well, but to the Gentiles. These were people with whom a pious Pharisee would not dare to associate. But God had made His choice.

From a human point of view, God's choice of instruments was so contrary to reason that it was hard to believe. Indeed, some refused to believe it. Saul entered Damascus to carry out his divinely appointed task. There suspicious whispers followed him: "Isn't he the man who raised havoc in Jerusalem among those who call on this name [of Jesus]? And hasn't he come here to take them as prisoners?" (Acts 9:21). He had no better luck in Jerusalem. There "he tried to join the disciples, but they were all afraid of him, not believing that he really was a disciple" (Acts 9:26).

If we were to stop reading Acts halfway through chapter 9, we might be tempted to think God had made the wrong choice after all. But by chapter 13 Saul, now called Paul, has become the center of attention. And by the book's end he is in Rome itself, the very center of the Gentile power. The last verse tells us what he's doing there. "Boldly and without hindrance he preached the kingdom of God and taught about the Lord Jesus Christ" (28:31).

## The Right Tool for the Right Task

As illogical as the choice of Saul may have seemed to observers, he was undoubtedly the right instrument for the task God had in mind. Reading through the Book of Acts you will observe that he founded churches throughout the Mediterranean world and converted a great many people to the faith. As you turn from Acts to the rest of the New Testament, you will see that Paul wrote nearly half the books in it. He was perhaps the greatest missionary the church has ever known. But who would have thought such a strange instrument could have such enormous effect? Well, obviously God did.

© DON MASON/CORBIS

**Who knows what sort of effect you might have as you give witness to God's grace?** God does. You're not so different from the unlikely Saul. God came to you in your sin and your rebellion, and He chose you to be His disciple. And in turn He's laid on you the task of making other disciples. You may protest and say you're ill-equipped. And you would be in good company to say so. Even Moses did the same (see Exodus 4:10). But as with Moses, God will not be rebuffed with feeble excuses. God's ways are not our ways; His thoughts are not our thoughts. But that is also the best news we could hear.

Our judgments would condemn people like Saul. And, if we're honest, people like ourselves. But on account of Christ, God has not condemned (see John 3:17). Instead, He has redeemed and remade us as His own instruments. It hardly seems logical. But it's the very truth. And a more wonderful truth you'll not find. ■

No matter how ill-equipped you feel, God calls you to serve Him and others through the Gospel. Sharing the Gospel need not start—as it did for Paul—in the synagogues and marketplaces of Asia and Europe. You are God's chosen instrument now, wherever you may be.